THE
FUNNIEST
TENNIS
QUOTES...
EVER!

Also available

The Funniest Liverpool Quotes... Ever!
The Funniest Chelsea Quotes... Ever!
The Funniest West Ham Quotes... Ever!
The Funniest Spurs Quotes... Ever!
The Funniest Arsenal Quotes... Ever!
The Funniest Man City Quotes... Ever!
The Funniest Newcastle Quotes... Ever!
The Funniest United Quotes... Ever!
The Funniest Leeds Quotes... Ever!
The Funniest Boro Quotes... Ever!
The Funniest Forest Quotes... Ever!
The Funniest Sunderland Quotes... Ever!
The Funniest Leicester Quotes... Ever!
The Funniest Saints Quotes... Ever!
The Funniest Everton Quotes... Ever!
The Funniest Villa Quotes... Ever!
The Funniest QPR Quotes... Ever!
The Funniest Celtic Quotes... Ever!
The Funniest Rangers Quotes... Ever!
The Funniest England Quotes... Ever!

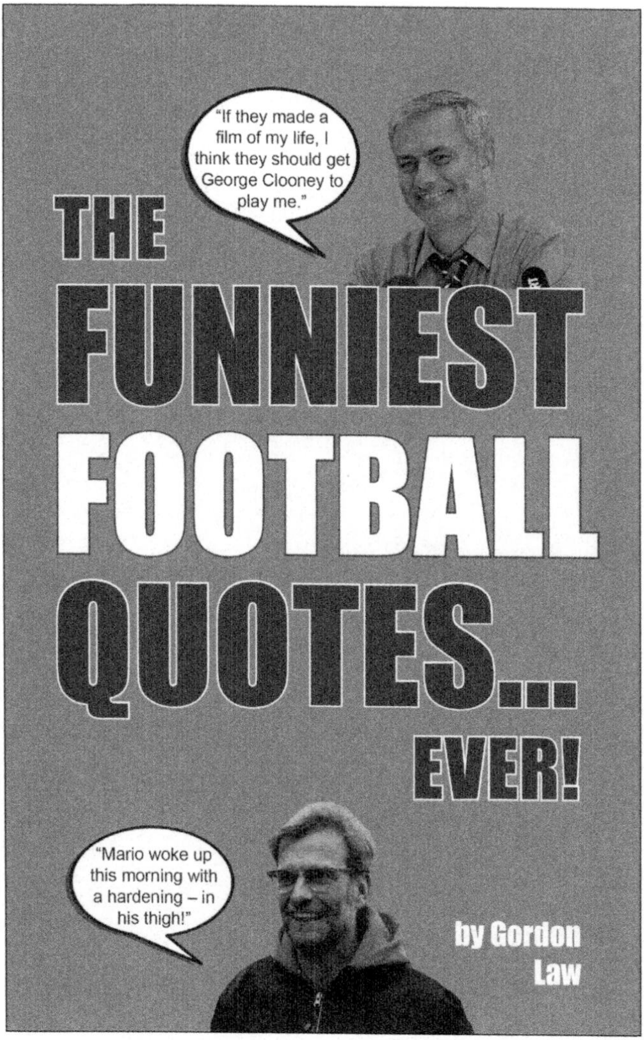
"If they made a film of my life, I think they should get George Clooney to play me."
THE
FUNNIEST
FOOTBALL
QUOTES...
EVER!
"Mario woke up this morning with a hardening – in his thigh!"
by Gordon Law

Printed in Europe and the USA

ISBN: 9798514736812
Imprint: Independently published

Photos courtesy of: Bart Sherkow/Shutterstock.com; Leonard Zhukovsky/Shutterstock.com

Contents

THE FUNNIEST TENNIS QUOTES... EVER!

VERBAL VOLLEYS

"I swear there is more bitchiness in men's tennis than women's. I don't like Djokovic that much. We know each other since I'm 12. He was a normal guy then, but since his first big success he changed, his eyes changed."

Ernests Gulbis on Novak Djokovic

"I think both of our worst nightmares would be to wake up the next morning and be the other."

Andre Agassi on Pete Sampras

"I threw the kitchen sink at him but he went to the bathroom and got his tub."

Andy Roddick after defeat to Roger Federer

"Get your fat a*se out of my way."

Marcelo Rios to Monica Seles in the Wimbledon players' dining room

"Last year I lost to his brother [John], this year I lose to him. Next year, maybe I can win against his sister."

Goran Ivanisevic after his defeat to Patrick McEnroe in 1993

"His day is done and now we're doing it. And we're doing it pretty well and not with fingers in the air and our hands on our crotches."

Jim Courier after Jimmy Connors claimed the top players were dull

"I'll follow that son of a b*tch to the ends of the earth. Every tournament he plays, I'll be waiting. Everywhere he turns, he'll see my shadow."
Jimmy Connors on Bjorn Borg after he lost to the Swede in the 1978 Wimbledon final

"Musumba Bwayla, my opponent, is a stupid man and a hopeless player. He has a huge nose and is cross-eyed. Girls hate him. He beat me in a two-hour match because my jockstrap was too tight and because when he serves he farts and that made me lose the concentration for which I am famous throughout Zambia."
Lighton Ndefwayl taking his defeat with grace

"I respect Roger, Rafa, Novak and Murray but, for me, all four of them are boring players. Their interviews are boring."

Ernests Gulbis

Q: "What's the difference between you and Patrick Rafter?"

Pete Sampras: "Ten Grand Slams."

"He has one weakness. He can never say his opponent played well. That's why it feels good to beat him and that's why other players would rather beat him than any other player."

Bjorn Borg on Jimmy Connors

"We're out there busting our guts and he doesn't show a lot of respect at the end of the day. He tries to play down the reason he lost, giving no respect to the other player. And that is what really upsets me about him and the reason I try to p*ss him off as much as I can."

Pat Rafter hits out at Pete Sampras

"I would like to congratulate Roger [Federer]. He is laughing, he is an a*shole, but is OK."

Stan Wawrinka

"We're good friends. He has his friends and I have mine."

Bjorn Borg on Jimmy Connors

"Fred's extremely bright and hard working and didn't miss much as a businessman. But he's an opportunist, a selfish and egotistical person and he never gave a damn about professional tennis."

Jack Kramer slams Fred Perry

"John McEnroe was my idol. He was the player I really liked to watch, but as a person, I don't think too much about him. He says I only have one shot. That makes me a genius or that makes the other guys very bad… He gives everybody sh*t. Who cares about John McEnroe now… He's an idiot."

Goran Ivanisevic

"They're like Bart Simpson's evil twins."

Brad Gilbert on Jimmy Connors and John McEnroe

"Agassi couldn't beat my mum now. He's finished."

British Davis Cup captain David Lloyd in 1999 before Andre Agassi went on to claim five more grand slams

"Pete screams worse than a parrot. The only thing I envy him is his dullness. I wish I could copy his peculiar lack of inspiration."

Andre Agassi on Pete Sampras

"He's a bit anal, he thinks the whole world is against him and that everyone is screwing him on some level. He's always been like that and he always will be."

John McEnroe on Jimmy Connors

"It is probably one of my best wins, but best games? I don't think so. I have had some beautiful losses."

Ernests Gulbis after victory over Novak Djokovic

"I've got more talent in my pinkie than [Ivan] Lendl has in his whole body."

John McEnroe

"Who's Rostagno? Nothing personal but I could have had a harder draw. There's at least 20 guys tougher than him and I'm not planning to lose."

John McEnroe – before being defeated by Derrick Rostagno

"What a monster! I want nothing to do with him. All that money and he never has time to smile. He gives the game a bad image."

Yannick Noah on Ivan Lendl

"I don't know that I changed all that much. They just found somebody worse."

Jimmy Connors on John McEnroe

"Hate is a very strong word – I just despise her to the maximum level just below hate."
Former player and senior ATP official Justin Gimelstob on Anna Kournikova

"Kokkinakis banged your girlfriend. Sorry to tell you that, mate."
Nick Kyrgios claims Stan Wawrinka's friend Thanasi Kokkinakis had slept with his partner Donna Vekic

"Half come to see him win. Half come to see him lose. Half come to see what happens."
Ion Tiriac is not so good at maths when describing John McEnroe

"I think I beat Roger Federer because I ate scrambled eggs in the morning."

Ernests Gulbis

"Nobody should be ranked No.1 who looks like he just swung from a tree."

Andre Agassi on Pete Sampras

"[Ilie] Nastase does not have a brain. He has a bird fluttering around in his head."

Ion Tiriac

"You're not good enough to be that cocky."

Andy Roddick to Gael Monfils

"[Pat] Cash is not one of my favourite people. He's one of the most aggressive, obnoxious players. I don't talk to him very often and I'm not the only one."

Boris Becker

"Back and hip. Cramp. Bird flu. Anthrax. SARS. Common cough and cold. You know, he's either quick to call a trainer, or he's the most courageous guy of all time."

Andy Roddick on Novak Djokovic's injuries

Q: "Is Jimmy Connors really an a*shole?"

Arthur Ashe: "Yeah. But he's my favourite a*shole."

"The Argentinians practise on the court for two hours a day, then they must practise in front of a mirror for two more hours saying, 'I'm not guilty'."

Vince Spadea after a number of players tested positive for banned stimulants

Andre Agassi: "Let's see what you've got, big boy."

Andy Roddick: "Hair."

"Perhaps there was something about Gilbert that made me look into myself and think, 'Oh my God, can I possibly be that unbearable?'"

John McEnroe on Brad Gilbert

"Sure, on a given day I could beat him. But it would have to be a day he had food poisoning."

Mel Purcell on Ivan Lendl

"Pancho's no saint. But whoever saw a saint with a tennis racket?"

Pancho Segura on Pancho Gonzales

"He is a disgusting player. Even though outside of the court, an awesome dude."

Ernests Gulbis on Fabrice Santoro

"There's no place for Stich in German tennis."

Boris Becker on compatriot Michael Stich

"Most people still hate Lendl with a passion. It's not hard to see why. He was arrogant, and amazingly for a Czech guy who took American citizenship, unquestionably a racist."

Pat Cash on Ivan Lendl

"I've been compared to [Guillermo] Vilas for a while now. I don't know him. All I know is that he was No.2 and I'm No.1."

Marcelo Rios

"When I first saw Andre [Agassi] at age two or three, I didn't think he was going to be any good."

Pancho Gonzales

"I know what the others say, but I'm not that obnoxious. I am not a punk. I'm 5ft 10in, 155 pounds. I've got broad shoulders and I can pack a punch. Most of these guys are windbags anyway. If they ever try anything with me, I'll be to the net fast."

Jimmy Connors after a defeated Stan Smith opted to leave the court without his opponent

"A haircut and a forehand."

Ivan Lendl describes Andre Agassi

"I feel like he just wants to be liked so much that I just can't stand him."

Nick Kyrgios on Novak Djokovic

"I think Connors believes he has to hate everyone he plays in order to play better, and McEnroe hates just about everyone who can beat him. He used to hate Connors and me. Now he has to hate the top 50."

Ivan Lendl

"I don't think I can ever be that phony."

John McEnroe on Jimmy Connors' new nice-guy image

"I see him more often than my mum, actually."

Novak Djokovic on yet another meeting with Rafael Nadal

amazon.co.uk

Thank
you for
shopping
at
Amazon.co.uk!

Packing slip for
Your order of 03 December 2021
Order ID 203-2676111-5355514

Qty.	Order Summary	Bin
1	The Funniest Tennis Quotes... Ever!	
	Paperback, Law Gordon. B096LS1VHH : B096LS1VHH:	
	9798514736812	

We hope you enjoy your gift, and we'd love to see you soon at www.amazon.co.uk

"He's my polar opposite, like literally my polar opposite. And he's super salty."

Nick Kyrgios on Rafael Nadal

"Comparing Pat Cash to Mats Wilander is likening a crack in the wall to the Grand Canyon."

John Newcombe

"The worst pr*ck I ever met."

Ilie Nastase on Marcelo Rios

Q: "Do you design your own shirt?"

Rafael Nadal: "I am not Sharapova."

GIRL
POWER

"I'm not the next [Anna] Kournikova – I want to win matches!"

Maria Sharapova on being compared with her compatriot

"It's fine, I just have really wobbly ankles. I wasn't meant to be a ballerina."

Serena Williams after slipping at the Australian Open

"I'm not Venus Williams. I'm not Serena Williams. I'm feminine. I don't want to look like they do. I'm not masculine like they are."

Anna Kournikova

"I'm like an expensive menu. You can look at it, but you can't afford it."

Anna Kournikova

"I'm a competitor. Unfortunately, it's a war out here. If there's a weakness, someone's going to be attacked."

Serena Williams on beating injured sister Venus in the 2002 Wimbledon final

"I'm more relaxed at Wimbledon so maybe that's why I can express myself a bit more tennistically on the court."

Amelie Mauresmo invents a new word

"Everyone always looked upon me as the bad guy – as the woman with big muscles."

Martina Navratilova

"People criticise me for being arrogant [but maybe it's] because I'm a little smarter than the others."

Venus Williams

"I have a record against [Sara] Errani three times: every time I have a bagel. A bagel means zero. Before the match I was just thinking: 'Better don't eat a bagel today'."

Hsieh Su-wei on her secret to beating Sara Errani

amazon.co.uk

A gift note from Jorgen Ellingsen:

Alex, enjoy your gift! From Jorgen Ellingsen

Gift note included with The Funniest Tennis Quotes...Ever!

"People believe because I'm blonde, I must be stupid. But the blondes are the smart ones."

Anna Kournikova

"I was looking in the mirror today and my waist is still 28 inches. I think it's all because I have a large bosom and a large a*s. I have a large a*s and it always just looks like I'm bigger than the rest of the girls. I could lose 20 pounds and I'm still going to have these knockers and I'm going to have this a*s and that's just the way it is."

Serena Williams hits back at her knockers after winning the Australian Open

"That's why I'm playing with this tape on my shin. It looked so cute but once it started scratching me I was a coward and ran away."
Caroline Wozniacki makes up a story about being attacked by a kangaroo

"I still don't fear anyone. The only things I fear in life are cockroaches."
Venus Williams

"I'm really exciting. I smile a lot. I win a lot and I'm really sexy."
Serena Williams after winning her first Wimbledon in 2002

"I hope Beyoncé saw that!"

Coco Gauff after her Wimbledon win over Polona Hercog

"Martina [Navratilova] claims I tell the dirtiest jokes around – probably as a semi-revolt against my strict Catholic upbringing. And when I've become angry in practice, every four-letter word imaginable has graced these lips."

Chris Evert

"Why should I have to look ugly just because I'm an athlete?"

Anna Kournikova, aged 16

"If someone is outplaying me and her outfit isn't nice, I refuse to lose to her."

Serena Williams

"A copy is never as good as the original."

Anna Kournikova after the press started comparing young stars as "the new Anna"

"If someone says I'm not feminine, I say 'screw it'."

Rosie Casals

"I'm good from behind."

Daria Gavrilova

"I was just trying not to sing at the change of ends."

Laura Robson on music playing during changeovers at her first match on Arthur Ashe stadium

"I'm happy with my red knickers. I'll keep wearing them as long as I keep winning. For these two weeks it's going to be red, then it's a surprise after that."

Tatiana Golovin after flashing her underwear at Wimbledon

"As much as I would like to be a robot, I'm not."

Serena Williams

"I should stay on the court and dance?"

Agnieszka Radwanska on why she barely shook Sabine Lisicki's hand and left the court after her Wimbledon semi-final loss

"It's not really a shorter skirt, I just have longer legs."

Anna Kournikova

"Somebody just smack me so hard in my head that something shakes finally, and I put the cables together."

Dinara Safina on trying to find form

"Some people, the player's mother is younger than me."

Kimiko Date, aged 43

"I felt like I had been hit by a train."

Simona Halep on losing the first set 6-1 to Serena Williams in Australia

"I think James Cordon was watching me today as well. I spotted him midway like first set, and then spent the rest of the time trying not to wave."

Laura Robson on playing her second match at Arthur Ashe

ANYONE FOR TENNIS?

"I may have exaggerated a bit when I said that 80 per cent of the top 100 women tennis players are fat pigs. What I meant to say was 75 per cent of the top 100 women are fat pigs."

Richard Krajicek

"There are some guys, I'm sorry, with respect – they can't play tennis. I don't know how they got into the top 100."

Ernests Gulbis after falling out of the top 100

"The dumber you are on court, the better you're going to play."

Jim Courier

"Finally, I win this son-of-a-b*tch tournament, and I take my trophy and go all around the stadium, bowing to the people and giving the finger to everybody. Then I take my rackets and break them up in my hands. I throw them in the river, and I stop to play tennis."

Ilie Nastase on his Wimbledon fantasy

"In about 10 years every woman will play topless."

Anna Kournikova, in 1998

"I always hated tennis."

Andre Agassi, in 2009

"The chemistry of a tennis player is different from that of a painter. The artist is not judged as harshly. The artist does not win or lose every day in black and white terms as we do. Picasso did not have a 5-3 won-lost record with Van Gogh. But I have to live with my 5-3 record against McEnroe and try to see that the balance doesn't change."

Bjorn Borg

"Women's tennis won't draw flies."

Arthur Ashe, in 1970

"Tennis stunts your personal growth."

Martina Navratilova

"Wimbledon. It's like making love a hundred times to the most beautiful woman you ever saw."

John Newcombe

"So many of the girls are horrible. You begin to feel hated. I have learned that every time you walk on court they want to kill you. Why? Because they don't want me to get ahead. Because they don't like the attention I get. Because I have a personality. Because I smile."

Alexandra Stevenson

"In tennis, there has to be a winner sometimes."

Roger Federer

"I am enjoying the sport I've been playing since six. It's better than cleaning the streets of Moscow."

Marat Safin

"I liked it better when I could just pull them off their chairs and stick a racket down their throats. Players don't have one right anymore."

Jimmy Connors, aged 39, on umpires

"They are trying to turn us into money whores. It's obscene."

Multi-millionaire John McEnroe on the $6million Grand Slam Cup

"You just lie on a couch, they take your money, and you walk out more bananas than when you walk in."

Goran Ivanisevic on sports psychologists

"It's a pain in the a*s."

Marcos Baghdatis on playing another late-night thriller at the Australian Open

"Here, for the first few days it's like a zoo. It's like a million people running around, brothers, sisters, mothers, fathers, grandmothers, so many people. That's pretty much annoying."

Marat Safin on The US Open

"I think it's about time she stopped that non-sense. It's making me throw up. It's disgusting. She'd been writing about it on Twitter all the time. And I was practicing with him before the tournament and my mum was on the side. When we were warming up, I shouted across the net, 'Feli... take a picture with my mum, because she thinks you're beautiful'. She wouldn't."

Andy Murray is embarrassed by his mother ahead of his match with Feliciano Lopez

"In tennis, you can only lose. The other guy can't eat you."

Gustavo Kuerten

"Women should not be allowed on Centre Court."

Jack Kramer after a long ladies' singles encounter delayed his match

"An asinine, pompous, overstuffed bunch of little men trying to run a big sport. Anything I've said or done to them goes redoubled."

Bill Tilden on the USTA

"Nobody is blaming the linesman. Of course, he did make a couple of big mistakes. Really big ones."

Marat Safin

"If you can't organise something like that, you can't organise a tournament."

Jelena Dokic blasts Wimbledon organisers after her courtesy car failed to show up, forcing her to hail a taxi

"At Wimbledon, the ladies are simply the candles on the cake."

John Newcombe

"I am not playing Wimbledon because I am allergic to grass."

Ivan Lendl missed Wimbledon in 1982 and spent the tournament playing golf

"If you're on a centre court TV match and you go up and say point-blank, 'F*** you', that probably wouldn't fly too well. You're probably going to get fined. So you'd say it more like under your breath and hope they hear it but don't really quite hear it, if you know what I'm saying."

Andy Roddick on dealing with umpires

"She expects to scrape me up off the Astrodome floor. I will scrape her up. She is a woman and is subject to women's emotional frailties. She will crack up during the match."

Bobby Riggs before Billie Jean King beat him in their 1973 'Battle of the Sexes' match

"I've never met a great champion who couldn't
be an absolute b*tch."

Ted Tinling

"No broad can beat me."

Bobby Riggs spoke too soon

"Women's tennis is two sets of rubbish that
only last half an hour."

Pat Cash

"But that's what all of the real grunters say."

**Andy Murray when told his opponent hadn't
thought his grunting would annoy him**

"I know from experience that men's professional tennis, for all its white, upper-class associations, is also a haven of promiscuity and easy sex, as perhaps all male professional sports are."
Arthur Ashe

"You are next to God if you win. And if you lose, you are not next to the devil."
Boris Becker

"I call tennis the McDonald's of sport – you go in, they make a quick buck out of you, and you're out."
Pat Cash

"I was in the locker room recently with five top-10 players. Not one word was said in 20 minutes. As I walked out, I said, 'It was a pleasure talking with you fellows'."
Jimmy Connors

"I would like to thank the sponsor, even though I think it is a disgrace to smoke cigarettes."
Pat Cash after winning the Salem Open in Hong Kong

"I have never believed a woman can success-fully play the net."
Bill Tilden

"Wimbledon is the world's most boring tournament. There is hardly anything to do apart from tennis."

Nikolay Davydenko

"When I helped run the Pacific Southwest, which always had a top female field, I watched carefully and saw the truth. Namely that people get up and go and get a hot dog or go to the bathroom when the women come on."

Jack Kramer

"Play very bad, please."

Rafael Nadal on what an opponent should do against him

"Maybe we should just have a good old brawl, guys streaming out of the locker-rooms onto the court and picking sides and fighting in teams – Europe versus America."

Jim Courier on how to liven up tennis

"Oversized rackets are for women, old people and sissies."

Jimmy Connors

"I feel like a horse in a circus. Sometimes, I'm getting crazy because people come and see me, and they point their finger at me, 'Look! Look! Look how she plays'."

Evgenia Kulikovskaya

"Women are brought up from the time they're six years old to read books, eat candy and go to dancing class. They can't compete against men, can't stand the strain."

Gene Scott

"I'm not backing down from anybody. You don't play this game to win. You play to kill people out there."

Lleyton Hewitt gets a bit dramatic

"Tennis judges are usually frustrated tennis guys who didn't make it, or old people who want to be around the sport."

John McEnroe

"If anybody ever manages to get the female fraternity equal prize money with men, that person should be awarded a gold medal and then locked away for robbery."

Pat Cash

"There are not too many places where you step on the court and people are telling you to go get a job, you bum."

Andre Agassi on the US Open fans

"These people are animals. Rome is the asshole of the universe."

Vitas Gerulaitis after losing to Adriano Panatta at the Foro Italico

"We have no grass courts in Chile. I agree with players who say grass is for cows and playing football... but I will try my best at Wimbledon."
Marcelo Rios

"Ladies, here's a hint. If you're playing against a friend who has big boobs, bring her to the net and make her hit backhand volleys. That's the hardest shot for the well-endowed."
Billie Jean King

"I was thrown into a lake full of crocodiles."
Pete Sampras on dealing with fame after winning the 1990 US Open, aged 19

TALKING BALLS

"She said I looked cute in the shorts."

Andy Roddick explains how wife Brooklyn Decker got him to relaunch his career

"I fell on my butt, but I've got a big butt so nothing happened."

Nicolas Almagro after he slipped during the French Open

"I lost concentration. I saw a really hot chick in the crowd. Like, I'm being jarringly honest – I'd marry her right now. Right now."

Nick Kyrgios after his defeat to Roger Federer at the Laver Cup

"I never misbehaved because I was afraid if I did anything like that my father could come up and kick my a*s."

Arthur Ashe

"My body is perfect, no? Physically speaking."

Rafael Nadal is quick to clarify he was referring to his injuries

"It certainly beat milking cows back in Australia."

Roy Emerson reflects on his career

"I've only scratched the iceberg."

Andre Agassi

"Nothing can prepare me for this. I just hope I play well and don't poop my pants."

Blaz Rola before facing Andy Murray

"I still break rackets, but now I do it in a positive way."

Goran Ivanisevic

"They call me a tower, not like a building."

Juan Martin del Potro

"I used to carry on like an idiot. Now I think it's funny when somebody freaks out."

Roger Federer

"Everybody thinks my name is Jerry Laitis and they call me Mr Laitis."

Vitas Gerulaitis

"I do have a personality. The people that know me know that."

Pete Sampras

"Me, I'm not a complete nutcase. I'm just different."

Marat Safin

"If you want tantrums or comedy, don't come and see me."

Ivan Lendl

"I'd rather be No.2 in Chile and No.1 in the world. I don't care about numbers right now."
Maybe Chilean No.1 Nicolas Massu does care

"There was a typo in the book. I did math, not meth."
Andre Agassi on the uproar over the admission in his book of using crystal meth

"People think I am unemotional because my voice is flat and a bit boring. It is unfortunate but it is just the way it is. I've tried to change it but it doesn't seem to make a difference."
Andy Murray

"They've lost my page. Somebody ripped it out. But I'm the main sponsor for the tour! I'm the guy who paid the most fines, so they should give me respect. There should be a page saying: 'This is the guy who paid the most fines'."

Goran Ivanisevic after being left of the ATP players' guide

"Nobody likes me. And I couldn't care a goddamn stuff."

Jimmy Connors

Q: "Are you part of the non-gluten diet craze on tour?"

Roger Federer: "No, I have extra gluten."

"We should be making more kids, I guess."

Novak Djokovic on not dropping a set in his first tournament as a father

Q: "What will you do after your Wimbledon semi-final defeat?"

Milos Raonic: "Eat unhealthy."

"I'm not really a 90s guy. I'm more of a 50s guy."

Pete Sampras

"To be honest, I think bananas are a pathetic fruit."

Andy Murray

"Bob Kain couldn't create an image out of a bar of soap. I've had my image ever since I was a junior. You can ask the players that."

Vitas Gerulaitis on the marketing executive

"I was losing so much that I just had to do something about it. I didn't know what else, so I cut my hair. All of a sudden I started to win, so I don't want to change a thing now."

Feliciano Lopez on chopping his locks

"I have seriously thought about retiring, but that was on a good day. On a bad day, I've thought about killing myself."

Ivan Lendl

"Nobody beats Vitas Gerulaitis 17 times in a row."

Vitas Gerulaitis on why he didn't lose to Jimmy Connors after 16 straight defeats

"If you got the guns, go for it. I got two bread sticks sticking out of my sleeve. I'll stick with sleeves."

Andy Roddick is avoiding sleeveless shirts at the Australian Open

"The best doubles team is John McEnroe and anybody else."

John McEnroe

"Prince gave everything to [Maria] Sharapova and [it has] no money anymore."

Nikolay Davydenko on why he has no racket endorsement contract

"It'll certainly give the pigeons something to do."

Pat Cash on having his own statue

"I don't know who is tall. Postman maybe."

The 6ft 10in Ivo Karlovic says he has average height parents

"I'm a little crazy, but I try to be a good guy."

Ilie Nastase

"I have pain not just in one place – I have it in my famous a*s."

Rafael Nadal after losing his Australian Open quarter-final to Fernando Gonzales

"Rod-dick... I had years of psychological issues with that."

Andy Roddick

"So lazy, do something, so lazy you are. You were playing FIFA until 3am, what do you expect?"

Nick Kyrgios chastises himself after he hit a poor return

"I feel like I'm a little lighter in my shoes, it makes me kind of run a little bit quicker because I feel like a stud."

Andre Agassi on being in love with Steffi Graf

"I honestly have no idea what makes me so sexy. I am neither an Adonis, nor is my weenie hyper-dimensional."

Boris Becker

"The bright side is I don't have to pay the rent at my house for another week."

Tommy Haas stays positive after his Wimbledon defeat to Roger Federer

"I can cry like Roger, it's just a shame I can't play like him."

A distraught Andy Murray after losing to Roger Federer in the Australian Open final

"I'm not a monster. I'm not all bad. Maybe 10 per cent, I think I'm 90 per cent good."

John McEnroe

"Get me a beer now. Honest to God, get me one now."

Nick Kyrgios makes a request to a fan during a second-set meltdown against Kevin Anderson at the 2017 French Open

"When you're 26, who are you gonna listen to, Jagger and Nicholson or some old farts in the United States Tennis Association?"

John McEnroe after being scolded by the USTA for his behaviour before Mick Jagger and Jack Nicholson told him not to change

"I'm winning with such bad tennis – it's incredible!"

Gaston Gaudio during Miami qualifying

"If I win Wimbledon, I'm gonna get naked probably."

Novak Djokovic when told Goran Ivanisevic stripped to his underwear after his win

LOVE-ALL

"Virginia doesn't think anybody should beat her – including God."

Wendy Turnbull on Virginia Wade

"It's very pleasant to beat Maria... Why? Well, I don't like her outfit."

Alla Kudryavtseva on her motivation to beat Maria Sharapova

"She spends more time putting make-up on than the rest of the girls combined. Her wrap-around skirts barely cover her tennis pants, which barely cover what should be covered."

Pam Shriver on Andrea Temesvari

"A couple of times I thought I was playing a guy."

Lindsay Davenport on Amelie Mauresmo

"You won, but I am better looking and I fit in the market better than you do."

Anna Kournikova after losing 6-0, 6-0 to Martina Hingis at the Junior US Open

"If I ever lost to a 14 or 15-year-old, I'd die right on the court."

Pam Shriver before losing to 14-year-old Gabriela Sabatini

"I guess she should be cocky. She beat me three years ago."

Chris Evert on Hana Mandlikova

"If she wants to talk about something personal, maybe she should talk about her relationship and her boyfriend that was married and is getting a divorce and has kids."

Maria Sharapova responds to Serena Williams for some controversial quotes that appeared to be directed at her

"He was practicing with his shirt off."

Victoria Azarenka on how Rafael Nadal won her support for the US Open

"I thought ProServ did a great job marketing Tracy, especially given her personality and her public-speaking ability."
Pam Shriver on Tracy Austin

"He played like a woman."
Billie Jean King after beating Bobby Riggs

"I will never lose to that little [expletive] again."
Serena Williams to a friend – according to Maria Sharapova's autobiography

"She travels with her girlfriend, she is half a man."
Martina Hingis on Amelie Mauresmo

"She thinks she's the f*****g Venus Williams, and she's not going to move out of the way. That's it. I'm sorry she feels that way."

Irina Spirlea after the pair bumped into each other while changing ends during the 1997 US Open semi. Richard Williams later called Spirlea, "A big, ugly, tall, white turkey" and was forced to apologise

"I like her, but who does she think she is when she parades around like a queen at the French Open, so absorbed that she does not even notice hands holding out for autograph books."

Nathalie Tauziat on Anna Kournikova

"I always beat [Jelena] Jankovic so who do you think I want to play?"

Marion Bartoli when asked who she would like to face next

"She talks like she's Serena Williams. Who is she? She's just another player on the tour. Bartoli is going to get it tomorrow."

Jelena Jankovic responds to Bartoli's barb

"She's very pretty, but I'm sure she would like to change places with me if she could and have four grand slam titles."

Martina Hingis on Anna Kournikova

RACKET
RANTS

"You can not be serious!"

John McEnroe

"My son is better behaved than you. I'll bring him to play you."

Jimmy Connors to John McEnroe

"You're on live TV, you know. You look like a real moron right now."

Andy Roddick yells at a chair umpire at Indianapolis

"You are the pits of the world!"

John McEnroe to a Wimbledon chair umpire

"I just want to know why it took you so long to get a white towel. Took you 20 minutes for this one. 20 minutes. Oh, you brought me two. Thanks."

Nick Kyrgios shouts at the umpire because his branded towel wasn't white

"If you start behaving like a beast during the match, I will turn into a bigger beast and I will destroy you."

Boris Becker to John McEnroe

"If I could, I would take this f*****g ball and shove it down your f*****g throat."

Serena Williams to a US Open line judge

"Gilbert, you don't deserve to be on the same court with me. You are the worst. The f*****g worst!"

John McEnroe while losing to Brad Gilbert in the Masters tournament in 1986

"That's hilarious. If Rafa [Nadal] plays that quick, I'm retiring from tennis. [You're] the worst referee in the game... a f*****g tool."

Nick Kyrgios blasts the chair umpire who felt he was taking too long between serves

"Grow a spine!"

Andy Roddick shouts at the chair umpire

"If you keep that up, I'll just have to knock you out."

Bob Carmichael to John McEnroe during a doubles match

"Don't even look at me. You're a hater. You're very unattractive inside."

Serena Williams to the chair umpire in the 2011 US Open final

"I would have loved it sometimes if an umpire or linesman had just said, 'Look, p*ss off you little sh*t'. Maybe they should have had more of a go at me."

John McEnroe

"Kiss that before you do that to me... You son of a b*tch... Get out of the chair... You're a bum... Get your ass out of the chair... Don't give me that crap... You're an abortion."

Jimmy Connors to chair umpire David Littlefield after he overruled a line call

"You'll be sorry you hit me, you f*****g Communist a*shole."

John McEnroe after he was whacked by the ball from Czech opponent Tomas Smid

"We need a clown for this circus."

Roger Federer during a frequently miscalled match at the 2015 Mutua Madrid Open

"Bro, you are taking the f*****g p*ss, mate? The ball was this far out, no joke. No joke. What are you doing? It's so far long. What are you doing? Like, what are you actually doing up there? It was this far out. Bro, it's taking the p*ss. I refuse to play... Your hat looks ridiculous, also. It's not even sunny."

Nick Kyrgios gets a code violation for this tirade and then mocked the umpire's cap

"Excuse me. That ball was soooo in. What the heck is this? It was not out. Do I need to speak another language?"

Serena Williams to a chair umpire after a series of incorrect calls

OFF THE COURT

"There's always a chance, I guess, that I'll say yes... so keep 'em coming, guys."
Eugenie Bouchard responds to the marriage proposals she gets on social media

"I quit a lot of stuff in my life. For example, smoking, drinking, staying up late."
Ernests Gulbis on why he believes he will have a successful 2013

"I'm glad to be back. I went for a walk yesterday, and I must say I really liked the renovated pedestrian zone."
Martina Hingis on returning to home town Kosice for the first time since she was three

"When I have a Sunday off I love to eat lots of junk. My middle name is Piglet."

Maria Sharapova

"My breasts are really good because they don't sag. They are firm and perfect."

Anna Kournikova

"I love women. I think every man should have two of them."

Bobby Riggs

"My best surface is my bed."

Jim Courier

"I should have taken it up a long time ago. I don't understand the rules so I couldn't argue."
John McEnroe after losing a charity squash match

"I'm still a virgin. I do not let anyone have even a peep in my bed."
Anna Kournikova, aged 18

"Call me a typical American, but I love ham and cheese sandwiches. And not just any ham and cheese sandwich. My mother's is the best. I have often tried to make exactly this sandwich, but I never succeeded."
Andy Roddick

"I don't have to play. I just stand there. I say, 'I'm from China'."

Li Na strikes fear into her opponents at table tennis

"Sex doesn't interfere with your tennis; it's staying out all night trying to find it that affects your tennis."

Andre Agassi

"I like that the marijuana here is legal. I'm for that. Unfortunately tennis players cannot do that, but I like the way of thinking."

Ernests Gulbis on what he likes about Rotterdam

"I could drink Jack Daniels without stopping. In the [Bollettieri] Academy, it was tougher to get away with, but I enjoyed it because you weren't supposed to. I smoked pot, oh sure."

Andre Agassi

"Yes, and I have a helicopter, a submarine and a spaceship."

Ernests Gulbis on whether he travels in his father's private jet

"Sure, I've been on the Tube – I caught it to Eastbourne once."

Serena Williams

"When I'm 32? Hopefully I'll have made my mark with a few different movies, some scary ones and some comedies. I'm really funny, I have a great personality on the camera."

A modest Serena Williams on what she might be doing in 10 years' time

"Don't worry about me. I have my own thing. I've never dated a girl. I don't let her believe that she's my girlfriend."

Ernests Gulbis when asked if he was dating

"If I did as well on the court as I do off the court, I'd be No.1 by now."

Vitas Gerulaitis

"If you meet a girl, I'm not ready to go in relationship with her straight away, so it's like, what is in my mind? For every normal guy, in your mind is to get the girl in bed. As soon as possible. It all takes energy. In a tournament, I don't do that."

Ernests Gulbis

"I socialise. What do you want me to say, 'I've got no friends?'"

Laura Robson when asked if her career leaves her any free time

"I know nuns with better social lives than me."

Wendy Turnbull

"I have a lot of boyfriends, I want you to write that. Every country I visit, I have a different boyfriend. And I kiss them all."

Anna Kournikova

"She always wins. The problem is I can't always keep my eyes on the ball."

Andre Agassi on his tennis matches with wife Steffi Graf

Q: "Why don't you show off your cutlery collection to friends?"

Venus Williams: "The problem is, I don't really have any friends."

"I remember when Jimmy [Connors] and I went into confession and he came out a half-hour later and I said, 'How'd it go?' He said, 'I wasn't finished. The priest said come back next Sunday'."

Chris Evert on her ex-fiancé

"My only good result in 1997 was marrying Brooke Shields."

Andre Agassi

"It would be a nice place if you took all the people out of the city."

John McEnroe on Paris, aged 18

"It was great. It was great fun; a very funny time. But I'm never going to go to Sweden again. If you go out and meet some girls, and immediately you're put in jail, that's not normal. It was very funny, though. I think everybody should go to jail at least once."

Ernests Gulbis on spending a night in a Stockholm jail for soliciting prostitutes

"Sex gets in the way of winning."

Jim Courier after leaving Morgane Fruhwirth

"The worst part is keeping the other girls away. They think I'm about to get married."

Vitas Gerulaitis

Q: "Who is your favourite author?"

Andre Agassi: "Don't have one, I never read books."

"I haven't [met him] yet but I have long been an admirer of his hair. Great hair."

Andy Roddick on David Beckham

"I believe this bird came all the way from Belgrade to help me."

Novak Djokovic on his feathered friend

Q: "Who's your toughest opponent?"

Karol Kucera: "My former girlfriend."

"I named one of my dogs after him. He was someone I loved growing up."

Andy Murray on Lleyton Hewitt

"A woman's place is in the bedroom and in the kitchen, in that order."

Bobby Riggs before his defeat to Billy Jean King

"Actually I am a tri-citizen. I've got a Hungarian passport as well. Just add that into the mix, guys. I mean, I'm pretty much the female version of Jason Bourne."

Great Britain's Johanna Konta

"I'd want someone a little younger than that. She's what I'd call a pitching wedge. She looks good from about 50 yards away."

Pete Sampras on Barbra Streisand, who had a short relationship with Andre Agassi

"I'll be honest – beer and women hurt us a lot."

Rod Frawley on why the Australians aren't as successful as they could be

"I don't want a girlfriend now. They're hard work and they're very dangerous."

Mark Philippoussis, aged 22

"I like to go to church. It's so nice and peaceful inside. You come out and you feel clean. Everything dirty is gone."

Anna Kournikova

"Whoever stole it is spending less than my wife."

Ilie Nastase on not reporting his missing credit card

"Would you complain if the chicks wanted to go after you? It's nice having that image. I remember when women wouldn't look twice at me."

Patrick Rafter

MEDIA
CIRCUS

Journalist: "How do you feel after that match? Do you feel in good shape going into the quarter-finals?"

Tomas Berdych: "Sorry? Excuse me?"

Journalist: "Do you feel your form is good going into the quarter-finals?"

Moderator: "He lost. He's obviously got a lot of matches."

Berdych: "Does he know right, or is he trying to make fun of me?"

Journalist: "No. Sorry, sorry."

"Please don't make me cry again!"

Roger Federer to Sue Barker at Wimbledon, 2004

Q. "If you lose, what will happen? Will you take it as an experience? Will you kill yourself?"

Petra Kvitova: "No, I will not kill myself, definitely."

A bizarre question asked before a Grand Slam final

Novak Djokovic: "Many of you stayed this late, thank you."

Journalist: "We have to."

Djokovic: "I know you have to, but make it look like you want to."

The Serb greets the media who remained after his epic 5 hours, 53 minutes Australian Open final win

Q: "How do you feel about being the face on the official US Open car?"

Roger Federer: "I can't sleep at night. It is so amazing."

The Swiss star's sarcastic response

"I can't rationalise talking to press people because they're not rational people."

John McEnroe

Q: "What are your chances of winning the 2005 US Open?"

Andy Roddick: "As good as anybody not named Roger."

Journalist: "What's Pete Sampras' weaknesses?"

Michael Chang: "He can't cook."

Interviewer: "Why did it take you so long to come to the press conference?"

Marat Safin: "I have to take care of myself, also. Sorry. I have to make some massage, smell good, shower."

Q: "Is it a good thing for the sport that both you and Venus were knocked out of Wimbledon on the same day?"

Serena Williams: "Yeah, I'm super happy I lost. Go, women's tennis."

"Bye-bye, bye-bye, and bye-bye again. It's too many questions about what I'm going to do, why I'm retiring, and this and that. I answer the same question, I don't know, a thousand times. Just go on Google and you have the same answer."

Marat Safin gets fed up with reporters asking about his retirement

Reporter: "You used to win matches like that."

Jim Courier: "And you used to ask good questions, too."

The American after losing a third-set tie-breaker against Marcelo Rios

Q: "What do you put your lack of confidence down to?"

Andy Roddick: "It comes from playing like sh*t. Why would I feel confident right now? If that was the case, I don't think we'd be sitting here having this funeral-like press conference. It's just weird because, I used to like hit for a half-hour and then go eat Cheetos the rest of the day, come out and drill forehands. Now I'm really trying to make it happen, being professional, really going for it, and I miss my Cheetos."

"How can you report on tennis and not know that?"

Andy Murray after a US reporter asked him who Fred Perry was

"Whatever I said last year, just copy it. I'm sure it still fits."

Andy Roddick to reporters after losing in the 2006 French Open first round

"Well I found energy because I really like doing these interviews, because I get my childhood dream to be a pilot. I feel like a pilot right now."

Ernests Gulbis explains how he won his next match after beating Roger Federer

Q: "Was there anything not working today?"

Andy Roddick: "Yeah, I couldn't get cell phone service in the stadium this morning."

The American at the ATP stop in San Jose

"I did play well in Australia. I don't know where you were. Were you under a rock?"

Roger Federer blasts a reporter

Interviewer: "Last time, at Wimbledon, you said, 'Next time I may have to punch him'. Do you have a Plan B?"

Andy Roddick: "Hit his face by a racket."

After losing to Roger Federer

"It's not interesting today. I know you were closing your eyes to be more focused on what I am saying."

Rafael Nadal jokes with a journalist who had fallen asleep in the press conference

PUNDIT PARADISE

"When it comes to being just plain horrible, Marcelo Rios is the No.1 seed at every tournament he plays in."

Sportswriter Martin Johnson

"The best way to beat him would be to hit him over the head with a racket."

Rod Laver on Roger Federer before the 2007 Australian Open final against Fernando Gonzalez

"Lleyton Hewitt may not be the worst Wimbledon champion, but he is certainly the dumbest."

Ted Schroeder

"I just wonder if her dad did say to her when she was 12, 13, 14 maybe, 'Listen, you are never going to be, you know, a looker'."

John Inverdale on Marion Bartoli, which he later apologised for

"I had a feeling today that Venus Williams would either win or lose."

Martina Navratilova

"Laura Robson has just made the best possible start to her professional tennis career, she won the first set and lost the next two and is out."

Mark Pougatch

"These ball boys are marvellous. You don't even notice them. There's a left-handed one over there. I noticed him earlier."

Max Robertson

"As Boris Becker sits there, his eyes staring out in front of him, I wonder what he's thinking. I think he's thinking, 'I am Boris Becker'. At least I hope that's what he's thinking."

BBC commentator John Barrett

"Leyton Hewitt... his two greatest strengths are his legs, his speed, his agility and his competitiveness."

Pat Cash

"If Richard Williams had danced in front of me after I had lost to one of his daughters, I probably would have hit him. What he did was absolutely horrible and has no place in sports."

Martina Navratilova after the father of Venus went on the court following her 2000 Wimbledon final win

"She comes from a tennis-playing family. Her father's a dentist."

BBC commentator

"That shot he has to obliterate from his mind a little bit."

Mark Cox

"In what other sport do you play six hours of tennis?"

Greg Rusedski

"When Martina is tense it helps her relax."

Dan Maskell

"If you can't get near a radio, Henman's taken the first set."

BBC Radio commentator

"Tennis is one of those games like all other games."

Virginia Wade

"Martina Hingis is going through a part of her life which she has never been through before."

BBC commentator

"I wonder if the Germans have a word for 'Blitzkrieg' in their language."

South African tennis pundit Frew McMillan

"Miss Stove seems to be going off the boil."

Commentator Peter West

"I have a feeling that, if she had been playing herself, she would have won that point."

Bob Hewitt

"She never loses a match. If she loses a match, it's because her opponent beats her."

Pam Shriver

"Well, judging from his serves, [Magnus] Larsson will either win this match or lose it."

Eurosport commentator

"Sampras, in white, serves with baggy shorts."

BBC commentator Ian Carter

"You can always feel much better if someone endorses the call – even if they are wrong."

Virginia Wade

"I'm an American. You can't go on where you were born. If you do, then John McEnroe would be a German."

Martina Navratilova gets John McEnroe's ancestry wrong

"Billy Jean King, with the look on her face that says she can't believe it... because she never believes it, and yet, somehow, I think she does."

BBC tennis pundit Max Robertson

"Getting your first serve in is a great way to avoid double faults."

Ex-Aussie tennis star John Fitzgerald

"Sampras' heart must have been in his hands."

Sky Sports commentator

"It's quite clear that Virginia Wade is thriving on the pressure now that the pressure on her to do well is off."

Harry Carpenter

"The Gullikson twins here. An interesting pair, both from Wisconsin."

Dan Maskell

"Federer is human, but for how long?"

BBC commentator

"She changed coaches more times than I changed wives."

Nick Bollettieri on Laura Robson

"The only thing that could have stopped Nadal this year is his knees."

Chris Wilkinson

"Martina, she's got several layers of steel out there, like a cat with nine lives."

Virginia Wade

"Laura Robson... solid between the ears."

Virginia Wade

Printed in Great Britain
by Amazon